Diana
at 50

LIFE Books

Managing Editor Robert Sullivan
Director of Photography Barbara Baker Burrows
Creative Director Anke Stohlmann
Deputy Picture Editor Christina Lieberman
Writer-Reporter Marilyn Fu
Copy Editors Barbara Gogan (Chief),
Parlan McGaw
Consulting Picture Editors Mimi Murphy (Rome),
Tala Skari (Paris)

President John Q. Griffin
Business Manager Roger Adler

Editorial Operations Richard K. Prue (Director),
Brian Fellows (Manager), Keith Aurelio, Charlotte
Coco, Tracey Eure, Kevin Hart, Mert Kerimoglu,
Rosalie Khan, Patricia Koh, Marco Lau, Brian Mai,
Po Fung Ng, Rudi Papiri, Robert Pizaro, Barry
Pribula, Clara Renauro, Katy Saunders, Hia Tan,
Vaune Trachtman

Time Home Entertainment

Publisher Richard Fraiman
General Manager Steven Sandonato
Executive Director, Marketing Services
Carol Pittard
Executive Director, Retail & Special Sales
Tom Mifsud
Executive Director, New Product Development
Peter Harper
Director, Bookazine Development & Marketing
Laura Adam
Publishing Director Joy Butts
Assistant General Counsel Helen Wan
Book Production Manager Suzanne Janso
Design & Prepress Manager
Anne-Michelle Gallero
Brand Manager Roshni Patel

Special Thanks: Christine Austin, Jeremy Biloon,
Glenn Buonocore, Malati Chavali, Jim Childs,
Susan Chodakiewiez, Rose Cirrincione, Jacqueline
Fitzgerald, Carrie Frazier Hertan, Christine Font,
Lauren Hall, Malena Jones, Mona Li, Robert
Marasco, Kimberly Marshall, Amy Migliaccio,
Nina Mistry, Dave Rozzelle, Ilene Schreider,
Adriana Tierno, Alex Voznesenskiy, Jonathan
White, Vanessa Wu

Published by LIFE Books
an imprint of Time Home Entertainment Inc.
135 West 50th Street
New York, New York 10020

ISBN 10: 1-60320-219-6
ISBN 13: 978-1-60320-219-0
Library of Congress Control Number: 2011926130

"LIFE" is a registered trademark of Time Inc.

We welcome your comments and suggestions about
LIFE Books. Please write to us at:
LIFE Books
Attention: Book Editors
PO Box 11016
Des Moines, IA 50336-1016

If you would like to order any of our hardcover
Collector's Edition books, please call us at:
1-800-327-6388 (Monday to Friday, 7 a.m.–8 p.m.
or Saturday, 7 a.m.–6 p.m. Central Time).

LIFE

Diana
at 50

PAGE 1: Diana Spencer, in 1975, as she draws nearer
to becoming a Lady. *UPPA/ZUMA*

PAGES 2–3: On her wedding day, July 29, 1981, Diana is flanked
by her husband (right) and his brothers, Andrew (far left)
and Edward, while in front are rambunctious
children from the bridal party. *Patrick Lichfield*

LEFT: The Spencer family tiara, which Diana wore to be wed
at St. Paul's Cathedral and on many
formal occasions thereafter. *Spencer Collection*

A Slipper Made of Glass

As a girl, she dreamed of being a princess. She became probably the most famous princess in the history of the real world—only Cinderella, Snow White, Helen (a.k.a. Sleeping Beauty) or Belle (the Beast's beauty)

might rival her in renown. But she never, ever could have dreamed what the reality of being a princess was like.

A potent combination of good fortune, ill fate, her personal character, a poor match of a marriage, the times themselves and a swiftly evolving journalism landscape made Diana Spencer the public figure she became, a global superstar without peer. She was born to the aristocracy in 1961—in a house situated on one of Queen Elizabeth II's country estates, in fact—and raised in an archaic tradition that didn't ask scholarship of its young women but instead put a premium on them being proper and presentable: attractive catches for aristocratic young men. On paper, it might seem that she was perfect to marry into the royal family of Windsor, which was almost petulantly persisting in its Victorian ways and expectations even as the 20th century was rapidly closing in on the 21st. All sorts of culture clashes—societal and personal—fed the Diana drama, as we will learn in the pages that follow. Queen Elizabeth, her husband, Prince Philip,

and their son Prince Charles were invested in clinging to the past, to tradition, while glamorous Princess Diana was very much of the moment (including the media moment). She had been invited into their midst, and once she was there, well, the Windsors had no idea what had hit them. Resentments grew, many having to do with the fact that she was winning the people's love in a way the royals never had been able to. Charles and Diana's marriage was turbulent and probably doomed from the start, and yet it lasted 15 years.

Also adding to the tale was what might be called "the other Diana," the non-tabloid Diana, the woman who had been gifted with a common touch and a sense of empathy entirely foreign to the ruling family. This wasn't the fashionista of the drop-dead backless dresses or the star turns on the White House dance floor, but the Good Mum running barefoot in the parents' races during field days at her boys' school, or comforting a child whose leg had been lost to a land mine, or hugging an AIDS patient (in an era when many feared such a gesture, and no other Windsor

would deign so much as a handshake). Diana had an intrinsic talent for connection—for making the right gesture—and it is to her everlasting credit that she put it to use so often.

The Windsors misread the whole story. If they had only perceived in Diana's public persona their new, best asset, rather than viewing her as some kind of threat or affront, they could have basked in her fame and charisma. But at day's end, they missed the point and missed their opportunity.

The cameras were constantly focused on Diana, of course. It is always a boon, when assembling a book like ours, to find that in the childhood years, one of the parents (in this case, Johnnie Spencer) was a keen amateur photographer. Better still, his youngest daughter was Johnnie's most willing (and attractive) subject. So no chapter in the Diana saga is lean on pictures. Many of these images are wonderful, and several, including some from the magnificent Wedding of the Century, appeared first in LIFE's pages.

Speaking of that wedding: It is particularly fun to return to the special day at St. Paul's

Cathedral in this season, after we've just witnessed the splendiferous wedding of Diana's fine elder son, William, to Catherine Middleton at Westminster Abbey (a ceremony celebrated in another LIFE book that's out just now). It's a kick to compare and contrast. Wills and Kate, children of the newer age, met at an elite university where they both were good students, dated for the longest time, suffered no slings and arrows about presumed "purity," persevered in their earnest love in the face of enormous public and private pressure and made a mature decision to marry. That's what young people do these days.

The two weddings occurred 30 years apart, but when you look at them, and consider the expectations put upon Diana in 1981, the gap seems instead like centuries. Kate arrived at the abbey by car. Diana arrived at the cathedral in a Glass Coach, which looked for all the world as if it had been magically transformed from a pumpkin by Diana's fairy godmother.

But then, she had always dreamed of being a princess. She had, as a girl, believed in fairy tales.

Lovely Young Lady Di

In her mid-teens, Lady Diana Spencer, youngest of the three daughters of Edward John "Johnnie" Spencer, Viscount Althorp and 8th Earl Spencer, and Frances Ruth Burke Roche, was enrolled, as older sisters Sarah and Jane had

been before her, at West Heath, a boarding school for girls in Sevenoaks in the county of Kent.

West Heath was of a breed of institution that still, as late as the 1970s, was more concerned with educating young girls of the upper classes in the social graces—

Even here, with a portrait of her when she was so young, it can be said: Diana, *in happier days. Her mother would leave the family when the girl was six, and Diana was devastated.*

preparing them for suitable marriages—than in turning out scholars. This was well understood by Diana's parents and it was fine with the child. She was in no way a standout student, even by West Heath's amiable standards; she would fail her O-levels twice while enrolled. In fact, though pretty, tall and friendly enough, she didn't stand out much at all. The overall impression among classmates and teachers was of a girl who was fun but already possessed of that somewhat drifty aspect the world would come to know so well.

There was, however, one thing about Diana that was indeed special then and would remain so to the tragic end of her too-few days. It is the main reason why, on what would have been her 50th birthday, we choose to pay attention once again, and remember her lovingly.

Twice weekly, West Heath girls would be bused to Darenth Park, a large old hospital in Dartford serving the mentally and physically handicapped. The trips were made in the spirit of volunteerism, but truth be told, many of the students dreaded them. In Rosalind Coward's biography *Diana: The Portrait*, Sarah Spencer, Diana's oldest sister (six years her senior), recalled the unpleasantness: "I remember them opening enormous wooden doors like in a medieval castle—you know, the ones you'd have to take a battering ram to. It smelt of disinfectant and pee . . . you saw this sea of ill people just coming toward you . . . [T]hey were all people with mental problems, serious mental problems. We had never seen places like this. We were sheltered little girlies."

The hospital manager, Muriel Stevens, knew of the girls' disquiet. "It was intimidating to walk into that huge place with the level of noise and

Diana's ancestry was in the aristocracy. Opposite, clockwise from bottom left: In 1926, her paternal grandfather, Jack, 7th Earl Spencer, lifts Diana's aunt Lady Anne Spencer, at the Pytchley Steeplechase, not far from the family seat at Althorp; Diana's father, baby Johnnie, and his mother, Cynthia; the 1953 debutante dance of Diana's aunt Mary Roche (standing, left) and mother, Frances (right), with their parents, Baron and Lady Fermoy, seated; and Park House, on the royal grounds at Sandringham, where Diana was born.

to see some of the very severely handicapped people," she said in Tim Clayton and Phil Craig's book *Diana: Story of a Princess*. "Some of them would be in wheelchairs. Some of them would be sitting on chairs and needed encouragement to move to get off them." Others needed no such encouragement, and for the girls this was scarier still: "[T]hey were just so delighted to see these young people they would rush up and of course they would touch their hair, grab their hands. And if you're actually not used to it that can be very frightening."

Into this situation walked Diana, and she was instantly in her element. "Diana was never frightened," said Stevens. "She was extremely relaxed in that setting, which for a young person of her age was incredible."

Stevens continued her reminiscence: "That tremendous laugh! That joyous sound! And it was wonderful because you wouldn't actually know what she was laughing at, or have any idea at all what had amused her, but at the sound alone you would find yourself smiling, and as you got closer and you heard it more, you'd find yourself laughing."

Other times, you might cry. The girls were

11

asked to move the wheelchair patients about in a little dance as music played. Many of the West Heath students did so haltingly if not grudgingly, of course holding the chair from behind. Diana would stand in front of the chair, grab hold and dance backwards, smiling at her partner, who would be transported.

Empathy.

The writer and editor Tina Brown was talking to the English journalist and historian Paul Johnson, who had known the late princess, about this quality for her book *The Diana Chronicles*. Johnson, famously a Roman Catholic who often writes with a moralist's stance, said, "She thought

HULTON-DEUTSCH/CORBIS

12

When Johnnie Spencer, Viscount Althorp, wed Frances Ruth Burke Roche, daughter of 4th Baron Fermoy and Lady Fermoy, in 1954, the setting (Westminster Abbey, left) and the ceremony were sensational—as society expected. It is a measure of their travails and trajectory that, after a messy divorce, each would marry almost secretly the second time around, with Johnnie not even informing his four kids, which included youngest daughter Diana, seen opposite in 1963.

she knew nothing and was very stupid. She made it impossible to criticize her, because she'd say 'I am thick and uneducated,' and I'd say, 'I don't think you're thick at all,' because although she didn't know much, she had something that very few people possess. She had extraordinary intuition and could see people who were nice, and warm to them and sympathize with them . . . Very few people compare to what she had."

Empathy.

It was empathy, compassion and a very rare and unquestionably genuine common touch— "I'm much closer to the people at the bottom than the people at the top," she told the French newspaper *Le Monde* in the last interview she gave before she died—that made her, as Tony Blair declared, "the People's Princess."

How she came by this special ability to not only make a connection but inspire true affection is very hard to say.

The Honourable Diana Frances Spencer was born on July 1, 1961, at home in Park House, Sandringham, Norfolk. We understand such an address conveys little to an American audience, but those in the know in England would immediately ask, "Sandringham? *Sandringham?*" And the answer would be, "Yes, Sandringham." Park House was not on the quaint main street of the coastal Norfolk village but on the edges of the famous 20,000-acre estate—the thing that gives "Sandringham" a name—an estate that was (and is) owned by the British royal family. Johnnie Spencer and his family lived there at the time of Diana's birth. The Spencers, as it happened and as might be assumed considering this circumstance of proximity, went way, way back with the royal family. It is lovely to note that, today, Park House is the Park House Hotel, still on the royal grounds but no longer a private residence, rather dedicated to housing the disabled and their caregivers. Diana would love that.

But in 1961, Johnnie and his wife, Frances, were raising their family there, and adding to it with their third daughter. They already had Sarah and Jane, and there is no doubt that the advent of Diana was a disappointment to her father at least: He was anxious for a male heir to whom he could hand down his title and possessions, a boy

PA

Opposite and above are Diana and her kid brother, Charles, at Park House circa 1967, just when their parents' marriage was failing and their mother was about to leave. Charles would eventually become 9th Earl Spencer at age 27 upon his father's death in 1992, at which point he would also inherit the family seat at Althorp, where he lives today. He has renovated the estate and built a Diana mausoleum and museum on the grounds.

who would eventually become Earl Spencer, holder of the imposing Northamptonshire estate Althorp. Johnnie's dismay was never manifested toward Diana, whom he loved, but resentments were growing between him and his wife, who had earlier given birth to a boy who, tragically, did not live—plus the two girls. Frances would eventually deliver Charles, who is today 9th Earl Spencer. He was the young man who movingly (and provocatively, even defiantly) eulogized his sister Diana in Westminster Abbey in 1997.

So Diana's upbringing was top-loaded and frightfully fraught before she was old enough to know it. She was a babe in arms and her parents already had issues with each other. Her two older sisters, still girls, were being groomed to be eligible female catches for men of title, and her father was pushing for a boy. She grew up distraught. Who wouldn't?

Johnnie Spencer fancied himself a good photographer—perhaps he envied Lord Snowdon's talents—and Diana found a way into her dad's affections by posing for him. As said, she loved her father, and she loved her mother as well. And they loved her. But this was

In two photographs taken circa 1970, Diana's pose in the image on the opposite page is less accurately reflective of her state of mind than that in the family portrait above, where she is at far right, wearing a somber expression characteristic in several pictures taken in the months and years after her mother departed and remarried. The family unit that Johnnie fought for in court is seen here, from left: Sarah, Charles, the patriarch, Jane and Diana.

no becalmed Baby Boomer nuclear family. This was an upper-crust unit with certain members who aspired to even greater nobility than the Spencer name already conjured in the 1960s and '70s.

To put it quickly, simply and dirtily (in a way that we Americans can understand), the prestige came from the paternal side—the Spencers—and the money came from the maternal side—the Fermoys. Johnnie's ancestors had always been cozy with the throne: The first Duke of Marlborough was an ancestor, and in fact the Spencer children, Sarah, Jane, Diana and Charles, were related to King Charles II (reign: 1660–1685) on their father's side through four illegitimate sons. They were also kin to Charles's successor, James II (1685–1688), through an illegitimate daughter. Members of Diana's mother's family, a predominantly Scottish and Irish clan whose considerable fortune was in large part the bequeathal of an American relation, the heiress Frances Work, had been employed by King George VI (that *King's Speech* fellow), his wife, Elizabeth (best known as the cherry-cheeked "Queen Mum"), and his daughter (a.k.a. Queen Elizabeth II, the still presiding

UPPA/ZUMA

18

monarch). The Spencer girls, breeding and beauty taken into account, would be expected to marry high. The recent wedding of Diana's son William to Kate Middleton shows how much English mores have changed in only a generation: These two intelligent young achievers met at one of the world's great universities, fell in love and chose to wed. That's a typical smart-young-people story, with the added fact that Kate was what is known as "a commoner"—i.e., one not from the British aristocracy. When Sarah, Jane and Diana Spencer were in their adolescence and young womanhood in the 1970s and '80s, the rules were vastly different, and royals and otherwise grandly titled men were looking to wed societal peers. The Prince of Wales, who is traditionally first in line of succession to the throne and who happened to be Charles in this time frame, was required to seek a partner who was estimable, lovely and virginal. Believe it or not: This was not

three thousand years ago, it was a mere 30.

As it happened, Diana was preparing herself, and not always unwittingly, to be that woman. She was accomplished at swimming and piano, and she once won a school prize for being kindest to her pet, a guinea pig. She socialized with boys but was reticent in love. She devoured Barbara Cartland romance novels and imagined her own Prince Charming ("The only books she ever read were mine and they weren't awfully good for her," said Cartland herself in 1993). Diana fell in love with Charles from afar, and wondered if one day he might be hers—in much the same way girls once fell in love with Paul McCartney or do today with Justin Bieber (but, in fact, with a far more realistic shot at such an outcome). In 1975, she officially became, at age 14, a titled Lady when her paternal grandfather died and her father inherited his earldom. "I'm a Lady," Diana declared as she rushed down a corridor at West Heath. "I'm 'Lady Diana' now!"

If she was jubilant in that moment, she wasn't a happy girl. Her parents had divorced when she was eight, and she had been brutalized by the family split. The story at the time—and it remains the standard version—was that Diana's mother had entered into an adulterous relationship with the also-married Peter Shand Kydd (whom she would eventually marry), and that therefore Johnnie Spencer was awarded custody of the kids. On paper, that is true, but affairs at the time were far more complicated. Frances Spencer did not desert the family, as her children were led to believe, but desperately wanted to be with her daughters and son. During the acutely acrimonious divorce proceedings,

19

Though she won no academic prizes, there were things she was good at and for which she was duly recognized, including ballet; the excellent care of her guinea pig, Peanuts (opposite, in 1972); and swimming and diving. In the photograph at top, she is enjoying a sunny day at Park House; when her father inherited Althorp in 1975, he built a pool there for the kids. The color photographs on this page, including the one of Diana packed for her return to her first boarding school, Riddlesworth Hall, are from the Spencer family's private photo album. The great majority of the snaps were from Johnnie's camera as he was a dedicated photo buff. Diana's sad eyes in the moving-day picture say much, but to her father she was even more direct: "If you love me, you won't leave me here."

> *Lady Diana grew up in a country family that owned stables and horses, and she was given her own pony, Scuffle, here offering a smooch in the mid-1970s. Later, however, Princess Diana would not share her husband's keen interest in riding or other equine sports. This was certainly not the largest issue between them; it was just one more thing.*

crucial testimony was given by Frances's own mother—Diana's maternal grandmother—that Frances was an unfit parent. Several biographers have alleged that this older woman, Baroness Fermoy, so lusted after status that she had once prodded her daughter to marry Johnnie Spencer, and now publicly denigrated that same daughter so that her heirs might remain "Spencers." The entrenched beastliness of the British aristocracy endures in the modern age.

In any event, the Spencer kids saw their mother as a bolter, and were at least mildly surprised when, at the end of a weekend visit with her and her new husband on the island of Seil on Scotland's west coast, Frances cried. In 1976, their father began his own affair with a married woman, Raine, Countess of Dartmouth (who was Barbara Cartland's daughter). Johnnie married her after she obtained a divorce, and Diana and her siblings disliked this match just as much as they did their mother's to Peter Shand Kydd. Diana manifested her anger by being mean to her nannies, none of whom stuck with the family.

The Spencer girls, 1977: Sarah was gregarious, socially ambitious and a target of many men; Jane was smart and also out on her own; and Diana, just turning sweet 16, was more than ready to leave school behind. She would not join her father and detested stepmother at musty Althorp in Northamptonshire. She would, instead, with a head full of dreams, go to London.

20

HULTON/GETTY

"The One"

Diana had been born on the grounds of the queen's immense estate at Sandringham, but when Johnnie Spencer inherited his earldom he also inherited Althorp, the Spencer family seat in Northamptonshire.

So the new earl and his family relocated from Park House to this rambling centuries-old stone pile that had risen on the site of the ancient lost village of Althorp and was the centerpiece of a 14,000-acre country estate.

In November 1980, Diana is all-but-betrothed, and now the photographic portraits are made not by Johnnie but by Lord Snowdon, ex-husband of the queen's sister, Margaret. Diana is headed for the Palace—and the Windsors.

A long-ago ancestor, Sir John Spencer of Warwickshire, had bought Althorp in the 16th century with money he had earned as a super-successful sheep farmer. The Spencers' original red-brick Tudor home had been thoroughly redone in the 18th century by architect Henry Holland, and it was the Holland house that was handed to Johnnie in 1975. The current generation of Spencers was by then a broken family. The older girls, Sarah and Jane, were little impacted by the move; they were already largely out on their own. But Diana, even though she boarded at West Heath, now called Althorp "home," as did her younger brother, Charles.

Life had changed. The new house, though indisputably grand, was draftier, creepier. Since the 1950s, when the 7th Earl Spencer first opened the doors of Althorp to the public in order to get around tax codes, it hadn't been a strictly private family dwelling—and now Johnnie, to supplement upkeep, instituted paid tours. If Diana and her brother were at first stoic, they were less so after Lord Spencer remarried on July 14, 1976, to Raine, Countess of Dartmouth. Johnnie knew his kids had disapproved of the relationship, so he simply hadn't bothered to tell them of the wedding. The Spencer girls and Charles truly detested this headstrong woman.

Upon their stepmother's arrival, someone wrote in the Althorp visitor book: "Raine stopped play." Things would bottom out after Johnnie suffered a near-fatal brain hemorrhage in 1978 and Raine, while nursing him back to health, would not allow his own children to visit his bedside.

But in between Raine sweeping in and Johnnie's convalescence, there was a day at Althorp in November of 1977 that is worth recalling.

Diana, the dreamy romantic and Barbara Cartland addict, had loved Prince Charles—the very idea of him—since she was a young girl. Charles, for his part, had been vaguely aware of that young girl since she'd been a neighbor at Sandringham; he considered her, when he considered her at all, as one of the children who played with his younger brothers, Andrew and Edward, at times when the royal family was on holiday in the country.

Althorp is a quintessential English country estate, with an immense and forbidding house that contains sigh-inducing elegancies behind its closed doors. Actually, some of those doors were opened to the public for a fee by Diana's grandfather Jack, after such things became acceptable among pinched members of the aristocracy. Diana was at first sanguine about the family's move to Althorp in 1975, but into every life a little rain must fall, and she saw a personal hurricane sweep in the following year with the arrival of Johnnie's second wife, her new stepmother, Raine (opposite, with hubby 8th Earl Spencer in their opulent, art-filled digs).

Opposite: Sarah Spencer certainly seems interested in Charles's reading matter during their dating days; maybe it would have been better had she successfully snagged him, as the prince's obsessive bookishness became yet one more sticking point between Diana and Charles. But in the mid-1970s, even as Sarah pursued the relationship, the teenage Diana (above) already had eyes for the prince, and on a fateful afternoon at Althorp in 1977, Charles chose the 16-year-old kid sister to give him a tour of the fabulous gallery (right), which had been greatly built up by the girls' grandfather Jack.

In 1977, Charles, first in line of succession to the British throne, was without peer the world's most eligible bachelor. The Fleet Street press, having been transformed by the RMs—Robert Maxwell and Rupert Murdoch—was chronicling and speculating and insinuating on a daily basis. Who would be "The One"—the one who was sufficiently beautiful and elevated and pure to be the next queen-in-waiting? The English public, voracious newspaper hounds, couldn't wait for the latest scoop. The people thrilled when Charles showed up at a society event with a pretty young Brit on his arm, and were dismayed when he was linked to an American actress or one or another "Latin firecracker." Charles's great uncle Lord Mountbatten, who was his most-trusted adult counselor (his father, Prince Philip, being domineering in the extreme and not prone to explication), had urged the boy to sow his wild oats before settling down. Charles seemed only too happy to heed this advice, and oats were sown far and wide.

He dated, among many others, Lady Sarah Spencer, whom he formally met at the Royal Ascot House party in the summer of 1977, not long after his discharge from the Royal Navy. She was invited to Windsor and Balmoral castles among other places for a variety of events, and this news of course made the gossip pages of the tabloids. That was okay with Charles; he couldn't eat breakfast without press coverage of the crumpets and kippers, and so being speculatively paired with this daughter of the peerage was unavoidable and

27

EVERETT

A postmodern Mary Poppins: Diana in 1978 (opposite), just before departing Hampshire for the city lights, hangs out the laundry of Major Jeremy, Philippa and two-year-old Alexandra Whitaker, for whom she is nannying for £16 per week. The snapshot was taken by the family's former au pair Marion ter Reehorst, who remembers, "Diana was very sweet and giggly but quite shy and unconfident." Left: Still a pram-pusher in London, where her employers say she is the best. The kids adore her.

not entirely unwelcomed. Charles's mother, Queen Elizabeth II, thought well enough of the Spencers, and there was some betting in England, where folks bet on everything, that this might be the real thing. That Sarah might be The One.

During their relationship, Charles visited Althorp for a pheasant hunt. (An American might pause here to remark: Royal Ascot house parties, pheasant hunts—you can't make this stuff up!) Diana watched longingly from the sidelines as Charles, her father and their dogs marched through the plowed fields in search of prey. She was introduced to the prince, and managed not to melt. If Charles remembered Diana from earlier, it wasn't clear, but she now made an impression. A family friend later told *McCall's* that Diana, a spirited, long-legged 16-year-old, taught Charles "how to tap-dance on the terrace." According to *Time* magazine, Charles was taken with "what a very amusing and attractive 16-year-old she was." When it came time for a tour of the Spencers' gallery of Old Masters paintings, which included

several masterworks by van Dyck, Charles asked Diana to show him 'round—this after Sarah had told her kid sister to bug off. Years later, Princess Diana would tell her public-speaking tutor Peter Settelen that she had felt pity for Charles "that my sister was wrapped around his neck because she's quite a tough old thing." Lady Sarah would only be so wrapped for a few weeks more, because the prince called the whole thing off after Sarah dished liberally about their relationship to the frothing Fleet Streeters.

Charles, just turning 30, could not, of course, show any kind of attention to a 16-year-old girl from an aristocratic family. But he certainly left Althorp on that November day with a memory.

Lord Spencer, who died at age 68 on March 29, 1992, is buried in the Great Brington parish church, near Althorp. Diana is buried on a small island in the center of a lake at Althorp.

The great house remains open to the public in the summer, with all proceeds now going to the Diana, Princess of Wales Memorial Fund.

Diana left West Heath girls school without having passed a single O-level exam but having been awarded a prize for outstanding community spirit. She studied (using the term loosely) very briefly at the Institut

29

31

Opposite: The ultimate nanny-to-goddess photo, the very instant Cinderella is no longer a chambermaid. In 1980, Diana's boss at the nursery school urges her to pose for paparazzi laying siege. Diana does so, unaware of the backlighting. Charles, for once, isn't upset, saying he knew his new girlfriend had good legs, but that *good? The British public says, "Wowza!" Above: Pix going forward are made from afar with long lenses.*

Alpin Videmanette, a now-defunct finishing school in Switzerland where the coursework included cooking, dressmaking, the French language and skiing. Diana skied better than she cooked, but didn't like much of anything about the school and petitioned her parents to be allowed to return to England. They acceded, and Diana landed in London before her 17th birthday, staying first at her mother's flat in town (Mrs. Shand Kydd was usually in Scotland) and then later in a South Kensington apartment found for her by Sarah and bought with £50,000 in family money from an inheritance that was freed up with her father's permission. She would live there with three girlfriends as flatmates until 1981, after which she would move with her husband to a more luxe set of rooms.

So she was out from under Althorp and Raine, out from under school. She was a lovely teenage girl at liberty in the big city. What to do?

Well . . . shop!

And keep up those cooking lessons (at her mother's urging).

And maybe look for a little work.

In the first capacity she became a card-carrying Sloane Ranger, a societal subset of upper- and upper-middle-class young women of the late 1970s and '80s nicknamed for the posh Chelsea square where they hailed from, hung out, sipped Champagne or, yes, shopped. They were characterized—or satirized—as über-preppies, generally underemployed and somewhat proudly anti-intellectual. They had a fashion sense and a patois that marked them. They knew who they were, and they recognized Lady Diana Spencer as a queen among Sloanes.

If Diana was not expected by friends or family to make something of herself professionally, it was nonetheless supposed that she would do something with herself. She was okay with that. Ever since she was encouraged in dance by the famed Madame Vacani upon the great woman's visit to West Heath school (Vacani's legendary studio in Knightsbridge had long been the training ground for children of the highest upper classes, including Princesses Elizabeth and Margaret and a young Prince Charles), Diana had dreamed of becoming a ballet dancer one day. But although her

Above is a historical artifact, the society-page equivalent of Reagan and Gorbachev in Reykjavik (except that Ronnie and Gorby would eventually become mates): Camilla Parker Bowles (left) and Lady Diana Spencer enjoy the Amateur Riders Handicap Steeplechase at Ludlow, in which Prince Charles is competing on October 24, 1980. Camilla seems content that Diana is Charles's newest paramour, and perhaps she is even beyond content. Opposite: Still a Sloane Ranger.

These pictures could be filed under: Balmoral, in happier days. Diana came to hate the royal estate in Scotland with a passion, and never had any affinity for wearing wellies or participating in blood sports. But during her courtship, she pretended to be game. The photo opposite might well document her last-ever fly-fishing experience. That said, she and Charles were smitten in 1980, and their mugging above reflects a moment of genuine good humor, not consternation.

training and natural talent would serve her well at royal balls and when cutting a rug with John Travolta, Diana was headed for a physical height of 5 foot 10—much too tall to be a ballet dancer.

But not too tall to tutor, and an early job in London was as an apprentice teacher of children at the Vacani studio. She left after only three months. It's not clear why. She claimed a ski injury, but that story had various versions. Subsequent jobs included house-cleaning at her sister Sarah's flat (Diana was paid a pound per hour), hostessing at parties, working as a nanny for an American family in London and then as a nursery assistant at the Young England Kindergarten in Pimlico. If there is a through-line in her employment, it is children, and later testimony by the parents of several kids she worked with indicates that she was magical with and among them. She was charismatic and kind, sensitive and simpatico, energetic and—again—empathetic.

Her social whirl at ages 17 and 18 was active but in no way untoward; her three flatmates were sister Sloanes, and this quartet traveled in a society of pretty young things who went to the

Life in London: the glamorous and not so glamorous, the happy and not so happy. In early 1981, Diana is prepared to make a splash at her first official public appearance by wearing the sexy black taffeta Emanuel gown, seen opposite, to a charity recital at Goldsmiths' Hall. She delights the press corps but perturbs the Palace and enrages her fiancé. Meantime, daily, she deals with Fleet Street on her way home from work (right), where her flatmates are eager to ask: "What's the latest scoop?!"

expected places, danced to the expected music. Diana, as if saving herself for her still-imagined Prince Charming, avoided serious entanglements. She was among her set's last virgins standing.

Which would be a factor when Prince Charles started paying much closer attention in the summer of 1980 after he remet Diana, now 19, at the country estate of Commander Robert de Pass, a friend of Charles's father, and de Pass's wife, Philippa, a lady-in-waiting to Charles's mother. Their son, Philip, had invited Diana for the weekend, knowing Charles would be the guest of honor: "You're a young blood. You might amuse him." Diana watched Charles play polo at Cowdray Park, then all returned to the estate for a barbecue. At one point, Diana found herself sitting next to Charles on a hay bale. The conversation eventually wound around to Earl Mountbatten, who had been assassinated by Irish Republican Army terrorists the previous year, and Diana said to Charles quite earnestly, as she later confided to her chosen biographer, Andrew Morton, "You looked so sad when you walked up the aisle at Lord Mountbatten's funeral. My heart bled for you when I watched. I thought, 'It's wrong. You're lonely. You should be with somebody to look after you.'"

Charles was genuinely moved by Diana's words, and almost immediately their relationship changed—and raced toward engagement, which would be announced on February 24, 1981. Diana was dizzied by the prince's—*her* prince's—new attentions. Charles, almost certainly, saw a palatable and undeniably pretty answer to a dilemma.

There was so much that was very, very, very wrong with this pairing, and so much of what was wrong was in evidence before they wed. Charles's relationships, encouraged by Mountbatten (who meantime had been angling for Charles to marry his own granddaughter Amanda), were many— and included several adulterous liaisons with married women of the upper class. One of these women was Camilla Parker Bowles, whom he had loved for a long time and who would eventually become his second wife. Charles wasn't ready to forgo any parts of his lifestyle; in fact, given a choice, he probably wouldn't have wed Diana at all, surely not in that time frame. But his grandmother the Queen Mum and his intimidating father, in particular, were pressing him, vigorously asserting that Charles's position as heir to the throne came with responsibilities, and

37

SNOWDON/CAMERA PRESS

SNOWDON/GLOBE

38

that this Spencer girl (Church of England, young, probably fertile, seemingly without a past) looks to be the answer. Right now.

Diana certainly angled to become Charles's love, as many biographers allege; and she certainly must have been savvy enough to experience some disquiet and perhaps doubt during her betrothal; but just as certainly, she was a relative innocent in this game. Her biographer Morton (and therefore Diana herself) wrote that, for instance, she was unaware that the married Parker Bowles intervened—or did not—in Charles's affairs depending upon whether she felt the new female in question posed a challenge to her own personal relationship with the prince. She apparently felt Diana represented little threat.

So Charles proposed and Diana said yes. She moved into Clarence House, the London home of the Queen Mother, in preparation for the great day.

Everyone is excited in the late winter of 1981 as engagement pictures are made, including a touching depiction of Charles's and Diana's fingers entwined, with his signet and her sapphire (which today belongs to Princess Kate) dominant. The crowd presses in against the Palace gates (below) as the betrothal is heralded on February 24. Inside, Lady Diana peers out at the throng, as shown opposite in a photograph that seems ominous, portentous, ghostly—like something out of Dickens. What does Diana's next chapter hold?

BILL CROSS/DAILY MAIL/REX USA

Would she have done so, if she had known? Would she have done so if she knew that, only shortly into her marriage, she would be weeping as she overheard Charles say into the phone, "Whatever happens, I will always love you"?

TED BLACKBROW/DAILY MAIL/REX USA

The Wedding of the Century

Diana Spencer, as we have seen in her childhood pictures, was a cute, chubby-cheeked little girl. Lady Diana was a teenager who was teased by her siblings and friends for her occasional gluttony.

Indeed, when the mood was upon her, she could and would pack away the foodstuffs. Still, she was always growing upwards more than outwards, and her increasing loveliness, which evolved into true, world-class beauty, eventually

The date: July 29, 1981. The place: St. Paul's Cathedral. The stars of the show: Diana and Charles, the newlywed Princess and Prince of Wales. Their prospects: According to the rapt world audience, sensational. Privately, dicey.

42

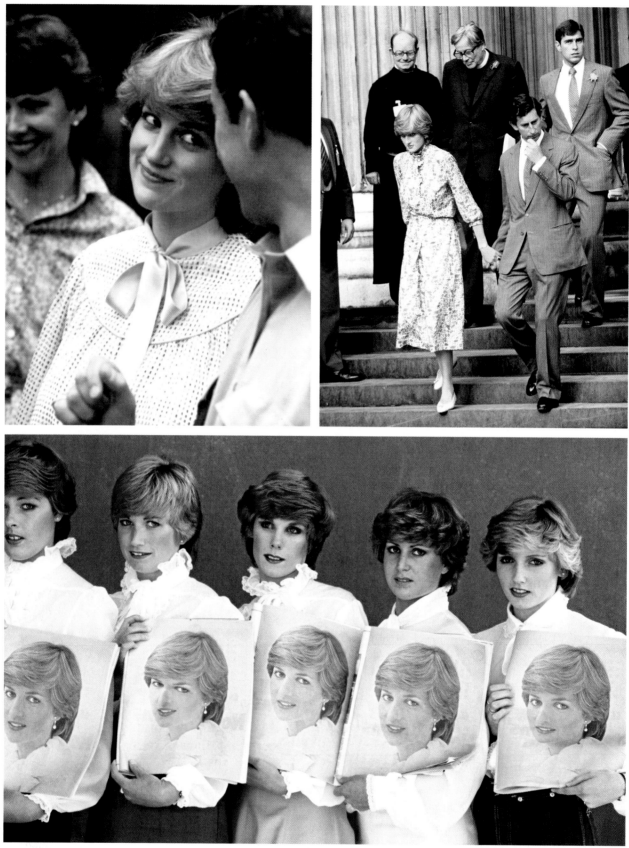

In the run-up to the big day, all eyes are on Di. Clockwise from top left: Five days and counting, she smiles for Charles; exiting their wedding rehearsal, the happy couple seem tired; five New Zealand misses pay tribute. Opposite: The Palace is deluged with requests.

became apparent to all. Her sister Sarah once remarked that, within the family, there was no talk through the years that Diana was en route to becoming any kind of goddess, while admitting that she sometimes heard comments from friends that this was happening. By the time Diana was linked to Prince Charles, most observers felt that he had chosen the most beautiful lass in the land.

But Diana's self-image regularly didn't match what was seen by her burgeoning horde of fans, "her public." Concerning "Shy Di," as the papers called her: She hadn't ever really been shy, though her lowered head and hunched shoulders tended to imply shyness in the paparazzi photos, but she was beset by insecurities. Stronger, older and more experienced women than Diana would have been affected by the pressure of an approaching role in the Wedding of the Century. Diana was not laid low by this pressure, but unquestionably she suffered under it.

She was only 19 when it all started, and barely 20 by the time it was finished. Charles was a dozen years her senior, a cocksure man of the world who was approaching his nuptials from an entirely different perspective than was his fiancée. He had been in an absolute torment about proposing marriage, writing to a friend in January of 1981: "I do very much want to do the right thing for this country and for my family. But I am terrified sometimes of making a promise and then perhaps living to regret it." After having put Diana through a hellish holiday season of silence, he finally pulled the trigger, and Diana celebrated her engagement girlishly. She returned to her flat in Coleherne Court and said to her friends, "Guess what?"

"He asked you. What did you say?"

Dear Prince Charles and lady Diand.

my greatest wish is to be brides maids to lady Diana. because I have never been bridesmaids and my sister Rebecca has. and I have been wanting to for ages.

Love from

Ella Carpenter

age 6

CLIVE LIMPKIN/DAILY MAIL/REX USA

"Yes, please."

They shouted and jumped like the Beatles had done in that Paris hotel room when they'd learned "I Want to Hold Your Hand" had gone to Number One in the States; then the girlfriends went out driving around in circles in London to burn off their excitement.

There was the briefest interim of relative calm between the February fact of betrothal and the public announcement, and then the maelstrom truly swept in, engulfing Diana. Even as just a candidate, she had been pursued by the Fleet Streeters, and had sometimes been found by friends in tears inside the doorway of her apartment building. Yes, true, conceded: Diana had, from the get-go, a preternatural gift for manipulating the media and having them adore her, as

43

Tina Brown and others have emphasized, but at some point the pursuit was so egregious and savage, no person—certainly no 19-year-old—should have been forced to endure it. Diana was forced to do so, and if Charles cared, he cared not much.

He did little in the period between the engagement and marriage to boost Diana's confidence, to shore her up for what was coming. As we learned in the previous chapter, he was ready to lay into her for questionable clothing choices (please see page 37), and at one point after withdrawing his hand from her waist he wondered at how "chubby" she seemed to be. When Diana looked at newspaper pictures of herself in her blue engagement suit, which she and her mother had bought at Harrods and which had elicited more than a mite of derision in the press, she saw herself as overweight. A season of tension-fueled bulimia ensued. As the rest of the whole wide world eagerly prepared for the glorious wedding—block parties were scheduled through Great Britain, invitations to midnight galas were sent out in Australia, the morning TV shows in America shipped convoys of personnel and matériel to London—Diana wasted away. "This little thing got so thin," her friend and former flatmate Carolyn Pride told Andrew Morton. "I was so worried about her."

The designers Emanuel had fashioned the scandalous black dress that Charles had so detested, but they retained Diana's favor; Elizabeth Emanuel was put in charge of the wedding gown, even though many at the Palace raised an eyebrow over the choice (as they did when Charles and Diana selected St. Paul's Cathedral over traditional Westminster Abbey as the site of their wedding). Between the first

fitting and the last, Elizabeth saw her client's waist shrivel from 29 inches to 23½. "Great anticipation. Happiness because the crowds buoyed you up," Diana told Morton about the lead-up to the ceremony, while adding quickly: "I don't think I was happy. We got married on Wednesday and on the Monday we had gone to St. Paul's for our last rehearsal and that's when the camera lights were on full and a sense of what the day was going to be. And I sobbed my eyes out. Absolutely collapsed and it was collapsing because of all sorts of things. The Camilla thing rearing its head the whole way through our engagement and I was desperately trying to be mature about the situation but I didn't have the foundations to do it and I couldn't talk to anyone about it . . . I had a very bad fit of bulimia the night before . . . I was sick as a parrot that night. It was such an indication of what was going on."

The sun comes up (or very often doesn't, not in any bright kind of way) very early in a London summer. On July 29, 1981, dawn washed over the city just after the witching hour, and the young and hardy who had camped out in the streets in order to secure good viewing places rubbed their eyes, as Diana did hers at five a.m. at Clarence House. The most dedicated of her public would be joined in London on this day by many thousands of her countrymen—600,000 celebrating outside St. Paul's Cathedral, 3,500 inside. For some, the work was done and the day represented, if not an anticlimax, a chance to savor triumph.

47

Opposite: Customarily, the father leads the bride down the aisle, but so unsteady is Johnnie on this day, the leading is left to Diana. Above: The Archbishop of Canterbury has a key role in the ceremony, but here Charles and Diana are bowing to the queen.

Lepidopterist Robert Goodden, whose company, Lullingstone, had prodded worms to spin the silk for Elizabeth's gown in 1947, had done the same, admirably, for Diana's Emanuel creation. Royal baker David Avery, in conjunction with Belgian pastry wizard S.G. Sender ("cakemaker to the kings") and others, was wiping the flour off his apron after helping create 27 wedding cakes, and was planning to "play golf, and lose myself for a week." Chorister Geoffrey Taylor and his 37 mates from St. Paul's had done all the rehearsing they could with a music program personally selected by Prince Charles—hymns like "Christ Is Made the Sure Foundation" and "I Vow to Thee My Country"—as had the Royal Opera Orchestra, the English Chamber Orchestra, the Philharmonia Orchestra and the New Zealand superstar soprano Kiri Te Kanawa. They were now primed and hoping for the best. In the event, they would all, of course, perform wonderfully.

Alarm clocks went off in New York City, dessert was served in Los Angeles, corks were popped in Sydney, TVs were switched on globally—perhaps a billion people would attend this event, one

*There are several—not enough!—photographs
like this from the early weeks and months
and even years of their relationship: sweet
moments of communion, and perhaps even
love. Here, Charles does not berate Diana,
but bolsters her.*

way or another—and Diana was dressed. "I was
very, very calm, deathly calm," Diana told Morton
about that morning. "I felt I was a lamb to the
slaughter. I knew it and couldn't do anything
about it."

It is well-known among dedicated royals
watchers that in 2011 Kate Middleton purposely
chose to arrive at Westminster by car for her
marriage to Charles and Diana's son William:
that Kate wanted to distance herself from
comparisons to Diana and, more important,
from the hoariness and grandiosity of certain
royal traditions. In 1981, the thinking was quite
the opposite. St. Paul's had been chosen over
Westminster in part because it was larger, could
fit more hundreds of people, and would neces-
sitate a longer, slower, more huzzah-filled parade
route to get there. Diana would make that trip
not in any kind of crass gas-powered conveyance
but in the *Cinderella*-esque Glass Coach, pulled
by two bays, including the legendarily purposeful
mare Lady Penelope, who could "take any procession in stride," as attested by royal coachman
Richard Boland. This was not merely pomp and
circumstance writ large. This was pomp and
circumstance in IMAX 3-D surround sound,
volume jacked to the max with a cherry on top—
and lots of whipped cream.

When Diana emerged from the coach, the
crowd oohed and aahed at her hitherto-top-secret
silk taffeta gown with billowing sleeves, bows,
lace flounces, sequins, pearls and a 25-foot train
that kept spilling out of the coach for what

50

Above: Man and wife. Opposite: Among the many, many fun things about this royal wedding is that stretch limos are out, and horses and coaches and carriages are in. Here, Charles helps his bride into the open-topped State Landau for their trip to the Palace.

In the pictures on this page, we see two small samplings of the 600,000 subjects who have filled the London streets to cheer for the newlyweds, and are now pressing in against the gates of Buckingham Palace to see what transpires on the balcony. Given his druthers, Prince Charles would have stuck with the hemming and hawing—oh, and one little kiss on the hand—seen in the first four photos on the opposite page. But at last Diana gives him the nudge, they lean in (seemingly unbeknownst to most other royals present) and . . .

seemed like minutes, as the clapping and cheering continued. The veil was of ivory silk tulle and glittered with 10,000 (you read that right) inlaid mother-of-pearl sequins, the whole of it held in place by the Spencer family's diamond tiara. If this is precisely what Diana had dreamed of back when she was a little girl with a headful of impossible wishes, well, this is precisely what she got. With the additions, of course, of a less-than-committed husband-to-be and his mistress-in-waiting on the guest list.

To be sure, Diana was on the lookout for her: "[W]alking

... whammo: the kiss seen—and demanded—around the world. For the historical record, it occurred at precisely 1:10 British Standard Time when the dithering newlyweds finally give the cheering public—and millions of anxious telly viewers globally—what they'd been waiting several pregnant minutes for. This was, for many Brits, the kiss of the century confirming the Wedding of the Century. Having got past that, the prince led his wife and family inside for a sumptuous celebratory repast with 120 very special invitees. Regardless of what the future held, this had already been a day to remember.

55

Right: A private moment, a precious picture. Thomas Patrick John Anson, the 5th Earl of Lichfield, better known publicly as the celebrity fashion photographer Patrick Lichfield, had been commissioned to be the day's documentarian. There were, of course, countless posed tableaux, with Lichfield stage-managing the scenes, telling kings and queens when to say "Cheese!" In the aftermath, however, it became clear that the best picture of all had been made when five-year-old Clementine Hambro—the great-granddaughter of Winston Churchill—bumped her head before being trotted out at the Buckingham Palace reception, and the ever-solicitous Diana, newly a princess, leaned over to console her. Lichfield grabbed a simple little camera from his pocket, and this lovely moment was captured forevermore. On the following pages: Dashing for the train, via landau, with escort.

56

down the aisle I spotted Camilla, pale grey, veiled pillbox hat, saw it all, her son, Tom, standing on a chair. To this day you know—vivid memory." That this should be a bride's personal takeaway from a wedding so many others enjoyed so rapturously is terribly sad, even tragic. But there it is, and was.

It is unfair to say that Diana was alone on the day of her marriage—certainly her father, though physically enfeebled, brought her forth, and her friends and other relations were in the cathedral—but a quick review of her team of bridesmaids and flower girls, many chosen and all of them rubber-stamped by Charles and the Palace, is illustrative of what she was getting into. The lead girl and therefore de facto maid of honor, 17-year-old Sarah Armstrong-Jones, Charles's cousin and Princess Margaret's daughter, was in the procession, and Charles's goddaughter India Hicks, and

They didn't necessarily meet their personal Waterloo at Waterloo Station. Perhaps they had already run up against it elsewhere in London, or maybe it would be more accurate to cite Balmoral as the place of ultimate reckoning. But in any event: Here the idyll ends, and the honeymoon from hell, of which we will learn more very shortly, begins. Whether Charles broke out his books on the train trip or waited until he and his wife were ensconced at the Mountbattens' Broadlands estate in Hampshire is lost to the winds of time, but he broke them out quickly. Very soon after playing her part in the Wedding of the Century, Diana began to feel alone in her marriage.

a daughter of one of Charles's close friends, and his racehorse trainer's daughter . . .

They all were lovely, done up by Emanuel so that they looked, as *The Times* of London put it, as if "they could have been plucked from a Victorian child's scrapbook." But they had come via Buckingham, not Althorp. When Diana's eldest son, Wills, married Kate just recently, Kate's sister, Pippa, was, officially, close by her side.

Famously, both bride and groom showed jitters during the ceremony, stumbling just a bit. During her vows before the Archbishop of Canterbury, Diana called her betrothed Philip Charles Arthur George instead of Charles Philip Arthur George, and Charles said "with all thy goods I share with thee" instead of "all my worldy goods I share with thee." No matter (and, in fact, quite charming), the ceremony was officially concluded, the music (yes, Elgar's "Pomp and Circumstance") swelled, the bells rang out and it was off to the Palace in the State Landau.

There, they appeared on the balcony at about one o'clock British Standard Time, before ducking back inside to host a wedding feast for 120.

The crowds pressing in at the gate shouted their only demand.

"I am not going to do that caper," Charles said to Diana. "They are trying to get us to kiss."

"Well, how about it?" asked Diana in return.

The prince paused and replied, "Why ever not?" He embraced his wife warmly, and even greater cheers rang out.

This was far better for Diana than the engagement announcement had been. Only five months earlier, an ITN TV interviewer, expecting an obvious answer, had asked the newly betrothed, "Are you in love?"

"Of course," Diana had answered with a laugh. Charles had offered: "Whatever 'in love' means."

ITN and other media buried the remark at the time, wanting to preserve the fairy tale that was unfolding before Britain's eyes to the delight of all. But Diana had heard her fiancé distinctly, and though she never asked him to explain further, she would always remember.

After much toasting at the Palace, Charles and Diana made their way to the landau, now decorated with a JUST MARRIED sign that had been attached by Charles's brothers, Andrew and Edward, and were driven over Westminster Bridge to Waterloo Station, where they would board a train for Hampshire and the beginning of their honeymoon. The Wedding of the Century was ended, but never to be forgotten. In 2011, even as everyone everywhere was buzzing about William and Kate, a stale, bite-size piece of Charles and Di's wedding cake that had descended from a sergeant in the Royal New Zealand Air Force sold at auction for $290. Many bidders had been drawn, as if to the original flame, by the romance of it all.

61

The *People's* Princess

TOM WARGACKI/WIREIMAGE/GETTY

*S*he was, in that instant in 1981, the world's best-known personage and arguably its most beloved (two distinctions she would successfully hold for the remainder of her days). Before she ever cradled a sick infant at a children's hospital

or comforted an AIDS sufferer at a hospice or showed herself as an exemplary mother to her boys, she was already the People's Princess (as British Prime Minister Tony Blair would formally dub Diana in the aftermath of her death).

It has been speculated that she was the most famous woman of the 20th century; she was certainly among the most photographed. Opposite: During a happy night out at London's Royal Albert Hall in 1982.

FROM TOP: PA/THE IMAGE WORKS; PA

Opposite, top: On July 29, 1981, the Waleses are hailed as their limo makes its way through Romsey, Hampshire, heading for Broadlands and the first stage of the multi-tiered honeymoon. Bottom: Three days later during Phase Two on Britannia.

Her grand and generously shared marriage ceremony had been a smashing success, her demeanor had been charming and mysteriously alluring, and now Diana's public knew no global boundaries.

And she was also, in that instant, thoroughly, entirely, grievously alone.

Her biographers take different tacks in their narratives and they take different sides, with the widest routes probably charted by Andrew Morton's constantly victimized Diana and Tina Brown's often crafty Diana. But on this they agree: The Charles-and-Di honeymoon was anything but. When did Diana know that it had all been a terrible mistake? When did she know it was already over, no matter what lay ahead? Most probably, by the second day. The second day of a marriage that would last for 15 years.

After the exhausting succession of Glass Coaches, St. Paul's and Buckingham Palace, the train from Waterloo Station took them to Broadlands in Hampshire, the estate of members of Charles's father's family. There, the multichaptered, three-month honeymoon would commence (and the relationship would be consummated, in the very bed once used by Elizabeth and Philip, although many assumed at the time and assume today that connubial relations had already occurred between Charles and Diana).

Diana told Morton of her first hours as Princess of Wales: "I never tried to call it off in the sense of really doing that but the worst moment was when we got to Broadlands. I thought, you know, it was just grim. I just had tremendous hope in me, which was slashed by day two. Went to Broadlands. Second night,

out came the van der Post novels he hadn't read [Laurens van der Post, the South African philosopher and adventurer, was much admired by Prince Charles]. Seven of them—they came on our honeymoon. He read them and we had to analyze them over lunch every day."

How does the old song go? *Isn't it romantic?*

We do want to stress here that we are seeking a balanced account, which is a thing almost impossible to achieve when recounting the saga of Charles and Diana, two ill-matched people whose relationship has, in its aftermath, been commented upon by each partner's passionate partisans, usually with a goal of slamming the other partner as culprit. When it comes to their affairs and missteps, we will try to be fair in these pages. In the case of the crummy honeymoon, however, it seems there's no doubt. The above passage concerning Charles's coldness is attributable to Diana via Morton. But here's Tina Brown, who is often skeptical of Diana/Morton's all-but-auto biography, writing in her own *The Diana Chronicles:* "To Andrew Morton she itemized all the particular acts of rejection by Prince Charles that were the cause of her desolation—the photos of Camilla that fell out of his diary as they cruised the Mediterranean on *Britannia,* his retreat into his solitary, highbrow reading, the cuff links from Camilla he wore in defiance of his new wife's feelings—but the really terrifying dimension to her grief was the sudden sharp understanding that all the things that had oppressed her during her engagement

64

Honeymoon, Phase Three: Balmoral. In August, the Scottish air is nippy, even frosty. For Charles, hand-holding by the banks of the River Dee eventually gives way to reading next to a favorite fishing hole, canine for companion.

were now her life forever. It was like an icy wave hitting her in the face. The oldness, the coldness, the deadness of royal life, its muffled misogyny, its whispering silence, its stifling social round confronting sycophantic strangers, this is how it would be until she died. Nothing else can explain the violence of her panic. As a former member of Prince Charles's staff put it: 'She saw she was going to become like the queen, possibly the loneliest person in the world' . . . When I think of the young, beautiful, newly married Princess of Wales at this time, I see her sitting up abruptly in the middle of the night in the Spartan spaciousness of her bedroom at Balmoral and uttering a long, bloodcurdling scream . . . "

To parse a few of the phrases above:

—The cruise on the royal yacht *Britannia* was Phase Two of the lengthy honeymoon, after Broadlands. "We had to entertain the boardroom on *Britannia*," Diana told Morton, "which were all the top people every night so there was never any time on our own. Found that very difficult to accept." As Brown reported in her book, 21 naval officers, a crew of 256 men, a valet, a dresser, a private secretary and an equerry were "sharing their romantic getaway" on the yacht. Yes, that might be very difficult to accept, and as Brown wrote further, with fine humor: "The trouble was that in this shipwreck movie there was no stowaway Leonardo DiCaprio to ravish Diana under the tarpaulin of a lifeboat. Instead, there was the Prince of Wales trawling his way through the complete works of Laurens van der Post."

—As for "the violence of her panic": On board ship, "the bulimia was appalling, absolutely appalling," admitted Diana. "It was rife, four times a day on the yacht . . . I remember crying my eyes out on our honeymoon. I was so tired, for all the wrong reasons totally."

—Regarding: "She was going to become like the queen." No, she wasn't, as we shall see. No way, no how.

—And finally: the imagined scream in "her bedroom at Balmoral." Phase Three of the honeymoon, beginning right after the *Britannia* had docked, was carried out as part of the royal family's cherished late-summer getaway at the queen's Scottish castle, and so now Diana's audience of midshipmen was exchanged for the far more austere and less friendly Windsors, including the queen; her husband; the Queen Mum; Charles's siblings, Anne, Andrew and Edward; Princess Margaret (Elizabeth's sister and Charles's aunt) and Margaret's two children; and on and on. At one point Diana asked Charles if, please, she could return to London. He said no. He told her to buck up. She did not, and it was noticed. One evening the queen commented to a dinner guest, according to Tim Clayton and Phil Craig in *Diana: Story of a Princess*, "Look at her sitting at that table glowering at us!"

In all past centuries, the royal family would have won: Diana would have been handed her head, figuratively or literally. But here was the rub for Queen Elizabeth, Prince Philip and all the others of Buckingham Palace: They and Charles had constructed this marriage on the ancient ways of doing things—the only ways they knew. These ways presumed, in any royal union,

67

Opposite: When pregnant in 1981, the exhausted princess began nodding off during sessions of Parliament (here) or at museum openings. The Palace, which would forever be tone-deaf regarding Diana, got it all wrong. They thought she should snap to it: buck up! The public saw her sympathetically.

evasions, suppressions and rueful acquiescence. But the royal family had found themselves— seemingly to their surprise if not astonishment— at the end of the 20th century, in a time where love affairs might well be conducted but might also have consequences; where marriages were entered into but sometimes led to divorces; and women might become complacent with their role or might find their own path.

The honeymoon ended after a lot of cruise control aboard the *Britannia* and then at Balmoral in October of 1981, and finally— finally!—Diana proceeded back to the city, to a new and fancier address at Kensington Palace (after a few months in Charles's Buckingham Palace apartment while the new digs were read- ied), where she would find not only her path, but her estimable, intrinsic—instinctual—and altogether marvelous talents.

Diana was so quickly and publicly pregnant after the wedding that even the cover story in *People* magazine, not the cheekiest or most aggressively provoca- tive of the world's many scoop-seeking weeklies, couldn't resist a little fun: "It seemed as though the rice had hardly been swept off the steps of St. Paul's before Britain was proudly atwitter over a new royal announcement: The newlywed Diana, Princess of Wales, is expecting to deliver an heir to the throne sometime in June. After a brief pause during which 'the nation's mums

counted on their fingers,' as one wry observer put it, the Buckingham Palace switchboard was jammed with congratulatory calls, hundreds of well-wishers gathered at the gates, and Fleet Street hailed the WONDERFUL NEWS in ban- ner headlines.

"The blessed event, if all goes well, will occur a prompt if perfectly proper 11 months after the July 29 wedding."

So at one point during the horrid honeymoon, between the princess's bouts of bulimia and the prince's sulky sessions with his mystical novels, something must have gone momentarily right, and the end result would mean all the difference to Diana. Motherhood was something the young Princess of Wales needed in this desolate period, something she could do, and, as it eventuated, something she could do very, very well.

She didn't have the easiest time getting there, as morning sickness was a constant. She was often fatigued, especially when she went out and about fulfilling her new, princessly duties. Oddly, her travail only served to boost her runaway popular- ity. When a photograph ran of Diana nodding off during a function at the Victoria and Albert Museum in London—a photo that was captioned the next day in newspapers worldwide "The Sleeping Princess"—the universal reaction was: "Ohhh, the poor dear!" Anyone who didn't love Diana was a cold-as-ice, heartless, soulless SOB.

Her first official, extended tour outside the city was a trip to Wales with her husband, where she wowed the crowds, meanwhile thoroughly (and completely unwittingly) dwarfing the man by her side, who was, after all, "the Prince of Wales." This was a harsh wake-up call not only

70

A new life. Diana was initially uneasy about being called Her Royal Highness; 15 years on, the title would be an issue in divorce proceedings (she lost it, retaining "Diana, Princess of Wales"). In Kensington Palace, stuffed animals help make it real, as does her diary. On the road, as in Australia (top right), there are now servants. Opposite: Working her side of the street in Wales in October 1981—already a pro.

for Charles but for the Palace: They had allowed someone into their stoical midst who, with her natural warmth and charm, would outshine them all in the hearts and minds of the masses— who would be revered in a way that they never had been and never could be. Diana, the young teen who had bonded with the mental patients and was, only yesterday, a modestly employed nanny and kindergarten teacher, put her practiced talents and innate empathy to use as she greeted a Welsh child suffering from spina bifida with a hug. She bent her knees, and looked into all the youngsters' eyes on their level. Although in highbrow royal arenas this simplicity might be considered a detriment, she spoke the children's language, she knew how to talk to them one-on-one in a mutually enjoyable manner. None of the Windsors had ever done these things or, frankly, had wanted to do them, or had even had the capacity or training to do them. Charles would later say that Diana taught him how to approach children in public.

If Diana, upon her return to London, was looking for a "well done!" from the queen or her prince—and there is no testimony that she was expecting anything of the kind—it certainly wasn't

As Prince William is born on June 21, 1982, fans and media keep vigil outside St. Mary's Hospital (above), giving only the barest hint of things to come. For decades—centuries—the royal family had been treated with decorousness, not to say kid gloves. But the very human saga of Charles and Di, coupled with the rise of press barons such as Rupert Murdoch who played by different rules, changed everything. Opposite: Outside the hospital, Mummy, Daddy and one-day-old Wills.

FRANCIS APESTEGUY/SIPA

TIM GRAHAM/GETTY

Others have written that if Charles had been truly in love with Diana—and he himself later said, in one of the semiauthorized war-of-the-Waleses biographies, that he hadn't been, ever—it might have been made to work. Certainly in 1982 at Kensington Palace, there was joy, as seen here. A quick word about Prince William, known to his family as Wills or, sometimes, Wombat: He would grow to be handsome and dutiful, and a successful student. He gained admittance to Eton College and then to the equally august University of St. Andrews in Scotland. There he earned the highest marks ever achieved by an heir to the British throne. At St. Andrews, Wills met and fell in love with his fellow student Kate Middleton. You might have heard: They wed on April 29, 2011.

forthcoming. Dr. James Colthurst, who as a teenager had met a younger Diana on a ski trip and had become a close friend, told Tina Brown that the result of the Welsh sojourn was that she "really got it in the neck from Charles." In their book *Behind Palace Doors*, Nigel Dempster and Peter Evans quote Stephen Barry, Prince Charles's valet, who had little use for Diana, as saying, "The princess had everything going for her except the ability to not upstage the prince." During a visit to Althorp in this period, there was a vigorous argument between the newlyweds in which a chair and window were broken—Charles was known to throw things when in a temper—and at one point Diana tripped and fell down a flight of stairs. Diana much later claimed to Morton that this was a suicide attempt, but at the time she had reported it as a stumble, and most biographers subscribe to the contemporaneous version. Would she actually have jeopardized her unborn child? That simply cannot be imagined of Diana, and as with other incidents in the Morton/Diana account, as well as Charles's post-divorce ripostes, there is revisionist history at play.

But enough, for now, of the painfully well-documented difficulties between the Waleses. Diana was about to give birth, and this buoyed her almost as much as it did her

TIM GRAHAM/GETTY (2)

76

Opposite: In the Australian outback in March of 1983, Diana descends—stunningly, and in not-exactly-suitable shoes—the iconic monolith Ayers Rock, known as Uluru in the Aboriginal language. Above: From Oz, the Waleses' road show continues on to New Zealand, where Diana appears to be having more fun than Charles. Following pages: A side story of the trip is that Diana has insisted on bringing the infant Wills, rather than leaving him in London with a nanny. Here, he is propped up by his parents in New Zealand.

countrymen. The punters placed bets on the salient question, and everyone waited with bated breath to know: Would it be a boy? Many cultures consider that an important point, but few care about the answer more than the Brits when the royal family's line of succession is about to be altered.

The blessed event occurred on June 21, 1982, in the private Lindo Wing of St. Mary's Hospital in the Paddington district, and word spread beyond the institution's walls, as *People* magazine reported: "The 41-gun salute at the Tower of London and Hyde Park signaled a king for the 21st century. The huzzahs rose across Britain, and eyes misted over from Land's End to John o' Groats. Well-wishers pressed to the gates of Buckingham Palace to read the placard that royal assistants hung out for the world to see last Monday eve: 'Her Royal Highness the Princess of Wales was safely delivered of a son at 9:03 p.m. today. Her Royal Highness and her child are both doing well.'

"The 7-pound $1\frac{1}{2}$-ounce prince is expected someday to rule the United Kingdom. He has already commandeered the attention of his future subjects from such concerns as the Falklands and

82

For Diana, the circuit now included official events, such as speeches at Restormel Farm in Lostwithiel, Cornwall, in May of 1983 (left) and lots and lots of polo matches. Charles's environmental causes and sporting pursuits never really interested her, but in the early years, she went along. Later, she responded to the outdoorsy/horsey scene with revulsion.

the Archbishop of Canterbury—who barely more than a year earlier had presided over Charles's and Diana's wedding vows—pouring the baptismal water on Wills's sensitive head and eliciting from the infant three small squeaks. Charles wiped dribbles from his son's chin, while any medievalists in the audience were cheered that the baby's cries indicated the Devil had been driven from the boy's body. Elizabeth II joked of William's vocalizations: "He's a good speechmaker." Charles's self-deprecating jape at the appearance of his first son was: "He has the good fortune not to look like me."

Charles would not reprise the line two years later when son Henry, known from the first as Harry, was born on September 15, 1984, also at St. Mary's.

"It's a boy!" a TV crewman announced on the latter occasion to the crowd of 300 reporters, cameramen and dedicated royals watchers who had been waiting outside throughout Diana's nine hours of labor for the birth of her second son. A cheer went up, and a rubbernecking motorist lost control of his car and crashed into an ambulance.

Diana had, in three short years of marriage, done her royal duty, providing "an heir and a spare"; her boys were now second and third in line of succession behind Charles himself.

"Three short years of marriage" that had at times seemed terribly long and borderline

Wimbledon. Even the newborn's father, normally the most serious of men, was transported. Charles, said his father-in-law, was 'absolutely over the moon.'"

Johnnie, Earl Spencer, also said: "The baby is lucky to have Diana as a mother. I'm off to have a beer." He was right about both Charles and the child—and where he was headed.

His Royal Highness Prince William Arthur Philip Louis of Wales (who, as we mentioned, only recently wed his own princess Kate in the most riveting royal wedding since his parents') was christened in the Music Room of Buckingham Palace six weeks later, with Dr. Robert Runcie,

And Harry makes two. Opposite, he is cradled by his mother, and at right, on his first day at Wetherby boys school in Notting Hill, west London, he looks up to his big brother, Wills, who will set an academic pace too fast to be equaled. The second son would not be a scholar but a sportsman and soldier, serving with distinction in the Afghanistan war.

unendurable. The fissures in Diana and Charles's relationship, which had been there from the first but had only grown worse, were now being insinuated by an increasingly prying press, and the extramarital affairs had been either reinitiated or begun in earnest. The consequences of these infidelities certainly would include the ultimate dissolution of the union, but what else? To this day, there is speculation that Harry, with his ginger hair, is Captain James Hewitt's son, not Charles's. The royals have bothered to say that DNA tests prove otherwise, and Hewitt, who has been routinely ungallant in reminiscing about his relationship with Diana—even unto cashing in—has said, in this case, that the when-when mathematics of their liaison and the birth don't work. But the DNA tests haven't been produced for independent examination, the mathematics are in dispute and the nattering classes carry on.

Even Harry's baptism in 1984, a celebratory event, put Windsor discord on public display and showed Diana in a me-against-them posture. The backstory: Charles was (and remains) close to his sister, Anne. Diana had few to no friends or allies in the royal family, and her relationship with Anne was sometimes chilly. *People* magazine, which had reported on William's christening with nothing but touching tenderness, was compelled to cover Harry's thusly: "[I]n London at year's end, it was the English royals—once models of at least surface harmony—who seemed

TIM GRAHAM/GETTY

85

woefully besmirched by bad tempers and rifts. In their fashion, of course, they struggled to be mum and mollifying about it all. But nothing could quite hide the rather awkward truth: While three-month-old Prince Henry Charles Albert David, third in line to the British throne, was ceremoniously baptized over a Victorian gilded lily font by the Archbishop of Canterbury in St. George's Chapel, Windsor, his Auntie Anne and her husband, Capt. Mark Phillips, were out shooting in the countryside, bagging rabbits.

"The real field day, naturally, was in the British press, which turned Anne's 'snubbing' of

The Good Mother: Diana found many downsides to being a royal, but an unquestionable upside was being able to vacation in splendid places, such as the Mediterranean island of Majorca, where Harry gets shod, opposite. Above: Diana doffs her own shoes and finishes strongly in the mothers' race at the Wetherby school's field day.

her nephew's christening into an apocalyptic—and apoplectic—event. How, they fumed, could Anne send her children, Peter, 7, and Zara, 3, but stay away herself? A feud in the House of Windsor, rumored for months, had finally erupted for all to see, crowed Fleet Street. Whiffs of grapeshot were first reported last October, when Prince Philip was said to be annoyed with Charles's lack of regard for his sister. Anne, 34, had not been named one of Prince William's six godparents at his 1982 christening. According to one senior royal aide, 'Prince Philip was very hopeful she would be chosen this time.' Yet when the list of Harry's godparents was published on Nov. 15, Anne's name was not among them."

Philip's ire (reputedly a daily thing) might have been directed at Charles in this instance, but really this was just the latest episode in Diana v. Windsors going wide. And neither Philip nor Anne nor

Charles was ever going to leave the family. Only Diana could, and insiders were starting to murmur that one day she might.

That day would not arrive—not technically, at least—for more than another decade, a decade that would involve a whole bunch of bad behavior, a multitude of bitter accusations, a million headlines, many books and much, much pain. Charles and Di began to lead largely separate lives before their marriage was five years old, but they also chose to soldier on. Finally, in December 1995, Queen Elizabeth had seen and heard and read enough, and advised her son and daughter-in-law to divorce.

B ut in the intervening years, of course, there were the boys to raise. Both parents loved their sons. What to do about that?

It has become increasingly clear in recent years that Charles

The flood of photos that would be captioned Trouble in Paradise starts now. Above: An undoubtedly playful moment that is irresistible as a visual symbol, wherein Diana breaks a stunt bottle over Charles's noggin during a visit to the set of the James Bond film The Living Daylights *in 1986. Opposite: No fakery, as Charles is perturbed that Diana has damaged his Aston Martin in June 1987.*

Keeping up appearances: The Waleses'
marriage is a sham, separation is being
considered, and yet a lovely family portrait at
Highgrove in Gloucestershire, a picture that
seems painted by Stubbs, is always possible.
The stiff upper lip of the British represents a
trait at once admirable and also mystifying—
a trait that the life history of the emotional,
confiding Diana put the lie to.

is a devoted father, but credit for Wills's and
Harry's upbringing goes to Diana. Early on she
asserted that she would be their mother in all
ways. She chose their names. She dismissed a
royal nanny and hired one of her preference (and
it can be imagined how that went down with
Philip and Elizabeth!). She dressed her sons,
planned their birthday parties and playdates,
selected their schools, and escorted them to class
as often as she could. She tried to remake her
own busy schedule of talks, hospital visits and
ribbon cuttings with an eye to their needs.

The kind of proactive mothering she displayed
was unprecedented in royal history. She took
them to McDonald's so they might feel like regular kids, and then she dragged them along on
her visits to hospitals in the hope that they might
learn about civic responsibility, and also absorb
some of her sense of empathy, which by now was
legendary and which she accepted as a talent.
The visits to the burger joints and sick-kids wards
had the desired effects.

As for royal and/or Windsor tradition: Diana
didn't seem to be very concerned with it. It's
too much to say "she couldn't have cared less,"
but if she was not overtly defiant of the Palace's
opinions when it came to Wills and Harry, she
was often dismissive of it. The boys would not
be circumcised, as British princes had been
since time immemorial, and they would both

attend Ludgrove School and, after passing their
entrance exams, Eton College. Windsor lads did
not go to Eton, they went to Gordonstoun. The
boys' father, Charles, had gone to Gordonstoun,
as had their grandfather, two uncles and two
cousins. But Diana's father and brother had both
attended Eton, and so would her sons. In short:
Wills and Harry were educated as Spencers,
not Windsors.

Diana's behavior, if not purposely rude, was
revolutionary and insurrectionist. To reiterate
the point: No royal mother or father, ever, had
deigned—no one had ever stooped—to raise a
royal kid in such a hands-on fashion. (Diana
winning prizes in the mothers' footrace at her
children's school's field day, for pity's sake.)

And then, good grief, it seemed to work!

The boys progressed beautifully, no matter
how hard prying eyes tried to find fault with
either them or their otherwise increasingly
tabloid-popular mother. Their boyhoods were as
normal as possible. The best the paparazzi could
do for the longest time was file photos of Diana
wiping ice cream off her sons' lips or of Mom
and the kids on a ski vacation in the Alps. Wills,
clearly, was as solid as the stone of Buckingham
Palace; he was smart and handsome, destined to
grow into something of a British JFK Jr. Young
Harry was a bit of a roustabout, even when Diana
was still alive, more into sports and tomfoolery
than his studies. The brothers continued on their
respective courses after her death: Wills, as said,
racked up the best grades at university of any
British royal in history (and the university in
question was the august St. Andrews in Scotland,
where, as also said, he met and fell in love with

PA

92

his eventual wife), then began his military career. Harry managed to pass a couple of A-levels at Eton, but pulled a D in geography while apparently majoring in polo and rugby. In 2005, he thought it would be humorous to wear Nazi garb to a costume party, which only pressed home for him (his mother certainly had warned them both!) that there are cameras everywhere—*everywhere!*—when you are an heir to the throne. That tabloid storm eventually quieted, and Harry's reputation would be largely redeemed with his service in the British army, in which he saw action on the front lines of the war in Afghanistan.

As the world watched the brothers perform so attractively at Wills and Kate's wedding on April 29, 2011, the general response seemed to be: "Good boys. Their mother's sons, of course." Whether this bothered Charles at all—and he certainly looked nothing but proud that day—it must have been noted by Elizabeth and Philip, who had always taken the general acclaim for Diana's renegade, modern mothering as an affront, an implied criticism of their own traditional, cold-fish, hand-shaking manner of raising

Shall We Dance, Part I: On the next five pages we see several pictures from 1985, one of which, perhaps, made Prince Charles happy. Opposite: He merrily escorts his wife in Melbourne during their second joint tour of Australia. Above: He chats with rocker/humanitarian Bob Geldof at the huge Live Aid concert for famine relief in London. Charles, who considered the event something his wife had dragged him to, was among the minority at Wembley wearing a suit and tie.

CORBIS

94

Shall We Dance, Part II: On November 9, 1985, Diana and John Travolta twirl at the White House for perhaps 10 minutes to tunes from Travolta musicals—and a moment is made that will live forever. Diana had thought she might trip the light fantastic with her tablemate this night, the ballet dancer Mikhail Baryshnikov, but he was suffering from an injury, and Nancy Reagan importuned Travolta, who later remembered the encounter as "a wonderfully special moment of her fulfilling a dream and giving me a new value . . . I looked her in the eye and said, 'We're good. I can do this.'"

PETE SOUZA/THE WHITE HOUSE

Diana at 50

97

Shall We Dance, Part III: One month after cutting a rug with Travolta, Diana slips out of her seat at the Royal Albert Hall with the intention of giving Charles a wonderful surprise present. A year earlier during the Friends of Covent Garden gala, she and her husband had performed a skit together, and now Diana, always a sensational dancer, would score points in their deteriorating relationship by partnering with ballet dancer Wayne Sleep in Billy Joel's "Uptown Girl." Whether Charles was upset at having been left out, or jealous of the thunderous applause cascading upon his lovely wife, is still unknown. But while the audience went wild, he did not—not in the same sense. As the suggested caption that moved with these images put it: "The future king was rumored not to have been amused."

J. BLACK/CAMERA PRESS (4)

CLOCKWISE FROM TOP LEFT: ALPHA/GLOBE; TIM ANDERSON/ALPHA/GLOBE; KEN GOFF; DAVE CHANCELLOR/ALPHA/GLOBE; PETER BROOKER/REX USA/EVERETT

99

Gal pals Diana and Sarah Ferguson (top left), and the Waleses at Fergie's marriage to Prince Andrew in 1986 (opposite). The next year, the princesses prowl at Ascot (top, center and right). The photos above are from the 1986 and '92 Remembrance Sunday observations. In the latter, Diana stands apart from Anne and the Queen Mum, and Fergie, now separated, has been erased altogether, as if by Stalin.

princes and princesses. The queen and her consort must have heard the readers of the *Daily Mail* sneering, "Well, look how Charles turned out compared to these two wonderful young . . . "

Three things bolstered Diana's public persona in the years that her marriage's fairy tale façade faded and as the transgressions of both partners were revealed one after another: her status as "the first one wronged," her reputation as an exemplary and loving mother and her dedication to helping the less fortunate.

The royals are always involved in philanthropic and humanitarian enterprises—it comes with the job—but they are just as always involved at arm's length, supporting charitable institutions and giving the haughty wave during hospital visits. Diana, by contrast, could never have told you how much money the Windsors had

On these and the next two pages we look at Diana the fashion icon; truly, you could fill a book (and others have). Opposite: At the Braemar Highland games in Scotland, 1982. The six above, clockwise from top left: London, 1982; at Michael Jackson's Wembley concert, 1988; London, 1984; two backless numbers in London, 1985; in Washington, D.C., 1985. Left, with Princess Anne on Derby Day, 1986.

FROM TOP: TIM GRAHAM/GETTY; MIRRORPIX/EVERETT

Creating a sensation was often a modus operan-Di. The blue silk chiffon strapless she wore at the Cannes film festival in 1987 (opposite, top) was no accident, nor was the distinctive veil she wore to Emperor Akihito's enthronement ceremony at the Imperial Palace in 1990. Right: Her most famous purpose pitch was the drop-dead black dress she wore to Vanity Fair *party at London's Serpentine Gallery on the night in 1994 when Charles's admission of adultery was to be broadcast on British television. This sexy number gave birth to the term "revenge dress." The Sun used precisely the headline Diana hoped for: THE THRILLA HE LEFT TO WOO CAMILLA.*

ANWAR HUSSEIN/LFI

103

contributed to a given cause, but she could describe in detail her encounter with the young, very ill girl with whom she had just exchanged a bedside kiss. She found her best self, exercised her best talents and cemented her relationship with the watching world by reaching out.

Some celebrities choose a cause because they feel, perhaps rightly, that they can accomplish more by focusing tightly: Bob Geldof and Ethiopian famine, Elizabeth Taylor and the fight against AIDS, Bono and Third World debt, George Clooney and Darfur. Diana didn't discriminate (and, it is not unfair to say, never really focused until late in her life, when she singled out the victims of hidden land mines as an issue—an issue that, certainly in part due to her high profile and dedication, would be acknowledged by the 1997 Nobel Peace Prize). Given the choice between fighting malaria or fighting drought, she might be conflicted (but she would enlist to fight both). Given the choice between a hospice visit or a night at the opera, an audience with Mother Teresa or a meet-and-greet with some grand duke from one or another vaguely Germanic principality—well,

her decision here was obvious. And, to the mind of Buckingham Palace, a bit bizarre.

Like Taylor, she became a champion of AIDS awareness. She worked to combat the scourge of leprosy. She assumed, in 1989, the presidency of the Great Ormond Street Hospital, an institution for children. This might have been the most meaningful of the many titles she held as princess, and she held it until she died. She traveled to refugee camps and soup kitchens. She fed the poor herself, holding the spoon. She was awfully good at what she did in this realm, and since a camera was ever-present, everyone, everywhere saw it—and was able to see the honesty of it.

MRS. E. WILSON/REX USA

The sad state of affairs. Camilla (left) looms over all. Charles's spurned wife eventually had a string of her own adulterous liaisons. Opposite, clockwise from top left: There is some question as to whether Diana's body-guard Barry Mannakee, seen here in 1985, was her lover, but there is no doubt that he died in a motorcycle accident in 1987 and the princess suspected foul play; the art dealer Oliver Hoare, seen at Ascot in 1986 just behind Charles, would not leave his wife for Diana; James Hewitt, accepting a polo trophy in 1988 as Wills looks on, carried on a five-year affair with the princess; James Gilbey (left) was Diana's second most famous boyfriend after Hewitt; rugby captain Will Carling saw his marriage implode after consorting with the princess.

104

So as a princess she was beloved as no other princess outside of fiction ever has been. But the final train wreck in her nonfictive personal life was rushing on, and in the early 1990s it occurred, as if seen in slow motion, hit by hit, screech by screech.

The tabloid stories about her lovers and Charles's return to Camilla were already on the table. But in a way, it can be said that it was Diana who declared war—or launched the first battle of the war's final stages. In June of 1992, Andrew Morton published his (and Diana's) biography, and her side of the story was now on the record. Charles's agents responded "off the record" or "not for attribution," and any rules of decorum were abandoned. It was no-holds-barred from

here on in. This was true for Fleet Street as well, of course, which had earlier made it clear that it was happy to flout such rules that others might think—ha, ha—still existed. The tabloid hounds started sniffing for ripe material, obtained by any means, and came up with plenty.

If 1992 was, as Elizabeth II declared in a speech that November, the queen's personal "annus horribilis," it was nothing less than that for Charles and Diana. What happened that year:

—In March, Charles's brother Andrew and his wife, Diana's wild-child pal, the former Sarah Ferguson, called it quits on the heels of the publication of topless photos of Fergie.

—In April, Princess Anne, Charles's sister, divorced Captain Mark Phillips.

—In June, *Diana, Her True Story* was published, detailing multiple infidelities in the Wales household.

—In August, taped conversations between Diana and her lover James Gilbey (the so-called

105

Why so glum? Well, why do you think? The photograph opposite shows the couple during another tour of Australia in 1988, well after each had begun carrying on with other people. Above: Still having to appear "together" during an official function in 1991 in Toronto. On the following pages: Same thing, in India, in 1992—the annus horribilis during which the Squidgygate and Camillagate tapes were revealed and so much other bad news rained upon the House of Windsor. The Waleses are entering their drawn-out endgame.

Squidgygate tapes, after an affectionate nickname Gilbey has bestowed on Her Highness) were published in *The Sun*.

—In November, Charles's Camillagate tapes, every bit as embarrassing as and even more graphic than the Squidgies *(I want to be your tampon),* were transcribed in two other newspapers, *Kent Today* and the *Sunday Mirror*.

—That same month, a major fire severely damaged Windsor Castle and claimed many of the family's priceless artifacts.

—Finally, in December, Charles and Diana officially confirmed what everybody already knew: that their union was no more and hadn't been happy for a goodly while.

Their announced separation after their years-old de facto separation did nothing to dim the spotlight. Paparazzi hounded Charles and Camilla daily, and doubled up on Diana and her new boyfriends.

Why the Waleses carried on for four more years—through increasingly brutal sequences of recrimination, embarrassment, and verbal and psychological assault, through further adulterousness, through a growing mountain of physical and emotional distress (for Diana, through many more episodes of bulimia), through periods of interpersonal battle that took a toll on their dear children—can only be ascribed to animus, or to the bogus

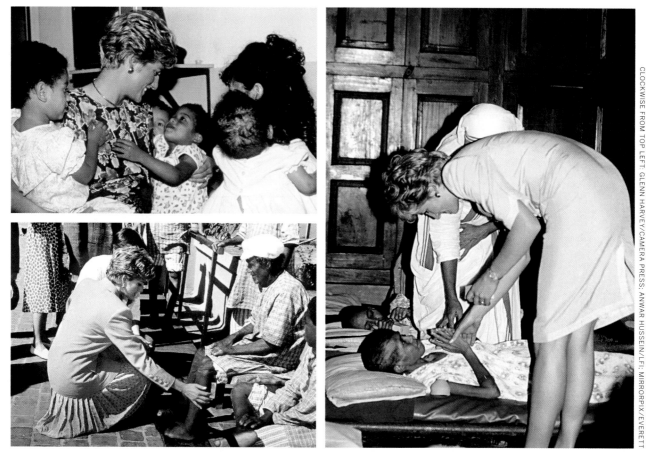

CLOCKWISE FROM TOP LEFT: GLENN HARVEY/CAMERA PRESS; ANWAR HUSSEIN/LFI; MIRRORPIX/EVERETT

110

"permanency" and "tradition" of the monarchy.

Consider: Even the great scandal of Edward VIII, which led to his abdication in the 1930s, didn't have to do with anyone divorcing him or him divorcing anyone, but with him wanting to marry a divorcée. The travails of Charles and Diana seemed, in the 1990s, much more consequential. Surely British princes and princesses had divorced in the past. Charles's Aunt Margaret comes immediately to mind. But first-in-line heirs to the throne had never been caught up in the kind of thing that Charles was caught up in—a thing he hadn't ever wanted and actually might have avoided, given a choice.

But it had come to this, at long, exhausting last, and on August 28, 1996, the Prince and Princess of Wales divorced, with Diana receiving a lump-sum payment of more than $30 million. The settlement included a standard clause in royal settlements: that details of the marriage not be discussed going forward.

Of course, the contract, at least that particular stipulation, had come much too late.

In this realm: a miracle worker. Above, clockwise from top left: Hugging children suffering from AIDS in Brazil in April 1991, a time when others looked at the affliction as a plague to be avoided; comforting a patient during a visit to Mother Teresa's hospice in Calcutta; reaching out to a victim of leprosy, yet another cursed scourge, in Nepal in 1993. Opposite: In February 1996, embracing a young cancer victim in Lahore, Pakistan.

JOHN PRYKE/REUTERS

The rift in her relationship with Charles was sufficiently longstanding that she often went her own way even when traveling with him; once liberated by their announced separation, she continued as Great Britain's top diplomatic superstar. Opposite: In Japan, in 1987. This page, clockwise from above: In Saudi Arabia, 1986; in Egypt, 1992; in Spain, 1987; in Hungary, 1990. Following pages: Charles was with her in India in 1992, but Diana famously posed before that ultimate temple of love, the Taj Mahal, solo. Today, this is officially the Diana bench, and tourists queue up to have their pictures taken on it.

Reaching Out, Racing Away

I n what seems an impossible calculus, Diana, no longer in line to be queen, grew even more famous. Only this particular woman could have engineered such a thing, and such a thing could only have been engineered in our modern age—

a golden age of celebrity, with tabloid journalism ascendant, juiced not only by hard-charging paparazzi and hard-digging ink-stained wretches, but by an exciting new electronic element.

Diana's earlier visit to Mother Teresa's hospice in Calcutta proved an epiphany, and a spur to her own efforts of mercy. In 1997, only two months before her death, she meets the saintly nun at the Missionaries of Charity residence in New York City's Bronx borough.

MIRRORPIX/EVERETT (2)

Diana was on Page Six every morning, *Inside Edition* every evening and, eventually, on the nascent Internet 24/7. For Diana junkies, and they were legion, Diana was omnipresent, omnipotent and, seemingly, omni-fascinating.

A most remarkable aspect of this phenomenon: She didn't really do anything except be herself. She had no profession. She wasn't a movie star, but was more famous than Julia Roberts. She wasn't a pop star, but was more famous than Madonna. It is statistically measurable that she was at least half-again more famous (and more popular) than her husband in the waning months of their marriage—in 1994, Charles's strategic TV interview drew 14 million British viewers, while Diana's rebuttal the following year attracted 21 million—and this held true when she was again single. She, who no longer had a job, a title or even a personal program beyond her day-to-day itinerary, might well have been the best-known person in the world.

What was this world looking for from Diana—what was the world asking of her—once she was divorced from Charles? Unfortunately, part of that answer is: scoop. What's the latest dirt from

Above, left: In January 1997, Diana dons a flak jacket and walks the land mine–infested terrain of Angola, in which country she meets and comforts many victims, including Sandra Tigica, seen in the photograph above, right, at the Neves Bendinha Orthopedic Workshop in the capital, Luanda. Opposite: In August 1997, now just days before her death, she is in Bosnia with the Landmine Survivors Network.

IAN JONES/ZUMA

the Buckingham Palace years? Who's the latest boyfriend? How's the eating disorder going? The answers to these questions, whether true or a million miles from the truth, sold thousands of newspapers and boosted the ratings of hundreds of TV shows.

The final months of strictly legal entanglement with Charles were as unpleasant for her as the honeymoon had been. At the end of 1992, British Prime Minister John Major lied to the House of Commons when he announced the Waleses' "amicable separation." Shortly thereafter the Camillagate transcripts popped up in the papers,

sullying the prince's image forevermore, and in 1993, Diana came to believe her husband was carrying on not only with Mrs. Parker Bowles but with Tiggy Legge-Bourke, whom the prince had hired to help care for Wills and Harry when they were with him. Another woman handling her beloved sons: That was quite enough. When Elizabeth suggested the marriage be dissolved, Diana was willing, though there would be much negotiation and legal wrangling. As the divorce proceedings dragged on, most of the public sided with Diana, especially when the BBC broadcast her 1995 interview with Martin Bashir (who

*In the late summer of '97, the al-Fayeds'
brand-new yacht was a supposed vessel
of refuge for Diana and her boys, but it
doubled as the principal target of the world's
paparazzi. Opposite: Dodi and Di are in
shades, William is squinting and Mohamed
al-Fayed is in resplendent green.*

would later get Michael Jackson to talk about his slumber parties with adolescent boys) in which Diana famously said, "There were three of us in this marriage." That quote endures today as something like the gossip page equivalent of "To be or not to be" or "Four score and seven years ago." The divorce was finalized on August 28, 1996.

So Diana was no longer Her Royal Highness, and was henceforth to be styled Diana, Princess of Wales. (It is enormously telling that, although Camilla Parker Bowles is today owed that title as Prince Charles's wife, she refuses to use it in deference to Diana's cult.) The Palace bothered to stress in 1996 that Diana, as a parent of the boys who were second and third in line for the throne, remained a member of the royal family—but such protestations represented semantics, technicalities, legalese. She was essentially persona non grata.

There was little doubt, however, that Diana would be allowed to keep her rooms on the north side of Kensington Palace and that she, the publicly esteemed mother, would continue to raise her boys when they weren't off at school. While there was no estrangement from their father, William and Harry continued as their mother's sons.

It is now known that other male presences at Kensington sometimes arrived hidden under blankets in the back seats of cars, or even concealed in the boot (as Brits call the trunk). Diana's social life became Topic 1A for the worldwide celebrity audience and therefore the celebrity press, and

some of the more serious-minded of Diana's paramours found the glare intolerable, even as they found the woman irresistible.

It is hardly elevating—in fact, it is pointless—to delve into this boyfriend or that one, or to make a list. But it is useful to visit, briefly, the case of Hasnat Khan. He was a Pakistani heart surgeon who carried on a love affair with Diana that lasted from 1995 to 1997. He was a man who mattered. And yet he was one who submitted to being smuggled into Kensington by Diana's butler/consigliere Paul Burrell, and who sometimes communicated with Diana via notes left at a pub near the hospital where he worked. This was a sober, intelligent man and . . . Well, what to say? It was all absurd. Dating Diana was a circus. Khan wouldn't allow the circus to progress to matrimony, so Diana was forced to move on from her relationship with him.

Finally, famously and fatefully, there was Dodi al-Fayed, scion in the family that owned Harrods department store in London, the Ritz Hotel in Paris and other interests. This was Diana's fling of the summer of '97, and few suppose that it would have gone anywhere. Dodi was a young playboy who had been encouraged in this escapade by his status-seeking father, and Diana was on the mend from the breakup with Khan. That's not necessarily a solid starting point for a stable relationship.

We say in the title of this chapter that she was reaching out, and racing away.

Reaching out: Diana remained a giving person to the end of her too-brief days, particularly in her lately assumed frontwoman position on the land mines issue; in January of 1997, pictures of her inspecting an Angolan minefield while

121

ANGELI/FAME PICTURES

Opposite: Diana, on the dash with Dodi (rear, left) during the fateful night in Paris, makes for the Mercedes. The paparazzi chased them from here, Dodi's apartment house, to the Ritz Hotel—then kept chasing as Di and Dodi kept running.

wearing a flak jacket put that cause front and center. Also, she and British Prime Minister Tony Blair had discussed a post she might assume as a humanitarian minister for the nation. It is said that, had she lived into the autumn of '97, she and the PM were going to sit down and figure this out. Yes, she was, as many biographers have written, at loose ends when she died. But she was looking forward to a sturdier, more tangible role in English society.

Racing away: She and the media had long been coconspirators, and if there had been occasional dustups, it must be admitted that both pursuer and pursued had relished the game for a good long time. Diana had always enjoyed being "Di." Well before she became a regular in the tabloids, she was a reader of them, and early on when her girlfriends reported back about a photo or article in which she had starred, she was pleased by the attention. Later, as princess, she was required to balance her affinity for publicity against the desires of her husband and the Palace. Later still, she sought to shield her children. So the once jolly game became a more complicated contest. After the divorce, it became something else altogether—a far more sordid enterprise. Consider this parade of trumpeted headlines from cover stories in issues of *People* magazine that were published between 1991 and 1997: "Home Alone," "Diana's Rival," "It's Over," "Diana on Her Own," "Battle for the Boys," "Diana's Lonely Battle," "Diana's Daring New Life," "Diana on the Edge," "Diana's Secret Lover," "Diana & Camilla," "Diana's Revenge: Take That!" "Di-Vorce!" "A Guy for Di" and "Goodbye, Diana."

Royals addicts can summon the stories from memory. Others among us, with what we have already learned, can easily fill in the plotline.

According to Hasnat Khan, it was Diana who called off their relationship late one summer night in 1997 while they were walking in the park. Why she wound up with the footloose Dodi al-Fayed within a month has been speculated upon endlessly. On paper, it looks like this: He was as rich as Croesus, and after her hoped-for summer vacation with Wills and Harry in the Hamptons on New York's Long Island was canceled because of security concerns, al-Fayed's invitation to holiday on the Riviera looked like an appealing option. Al-Fayed's father bought a new multimillion-dollar yacht, the *Jonikal*, so that the princess could be properly entertained.

Diana and Dodi spent nine days cruising the Mediterranean on the 60-meter boat in late August, then made their way to Paris on August 30. The evening that ensued was crazed in the extreme, with the two of them running from paparazzi, attempting a dining room dinner at the Ritz hotel, changing plans and supping upstairs, finally deciding to make a run for Dodi's apartment overlooking the Avenue des Champs Elysées. Accounts of those hours are as wildly varied as Diana's and Charles's versions of what went wrong between the two of them. They range from Diana being blissful about her fresh pregnancy and incipient engagement to Dodi to her being so overwrought and desperate to

be anywhere else in the world that she is openly weeping in a dining room at the Ritz. Dodi's father would later allege that their deaths were engineered by the British spy agency M16 on the orders of Diana's former father-in-law, Prince Philip—that's how nuts this all gets.

The proven facts are: At about 20 minutes past midnight, Diana and Dodi ducked out a back entrance of the Ritz and dashed into a black Mercedes-Benz. In the front passenger seat was Trevor Rees-Jones of the al-Fayed family's security team; he would be the only one to survive the crash. Driving, unfortunately, was Henri Paul, the acting head of security at the Ritz, who was under the influence of alcohol and prescription drugs and yet sped away at twice the legal

limit to outpace the trailing paparazzi. It should be noted: He was well clear of the pack when he lost control of the car three minutes later at the entrance to the Pont de l'Alma tunnel along the River Seine. The Mercedes hit a pillar and was demolished. Paul and al-Fayed were killed, probably instantly. Diana was not, but her internal injuries were such that, after hours of life-saving efforts at the Pitié-Salpêtrière Hospital, she passed away at four a.m.

England woke up to the news that Sunday morning and could not believe what it was hearing. The royal family was of course at Balmoral, since it was late summer. At this Scottish estate that Diana had never loved, Charles told his sons what had happened to their mother.

Aftermath
"We Love You, Diana!"

I t was slow to sink in that Sunday morning. "What did you say? Princess Diana has died? Diana is dead?" This was one of those where-were-you-when-you-heard? moments. JFK, MLK, RFK, the Challenger explosion. We all remember

where we were, and how unreal, entirely untethered, the next moments of our existence seemed to be.

The reality of her death didn't readily register, and the misjudgment of what it meant was

Few ever could have predicted the outpouring of emotion and abject communal grief that followed in the wake of Diana's death. If there's a measurement, it might be the sea of flowers that swelled outside Kensington Palace.

She rests today on this island in the center of a lake on the grounds of Althorp—a place of perfect peace. And for Diana at last, a perfect place of peace.

widespread. In no way was this cluelessness of its import the exclusive domain of Queen Elizabeth, Prince Philip and their coterie. Others beyond the royal circle wondered as the groundswell started: Hey, why such a big deal?

Tony Blair understood, and got it precisely right: "The People's Princess"—the first-ever such person in the history of the British Empire—had been taken from the scene.

The bouquets of flowers began to pile up at the gates of Buckingham Palace and at the entrance to Kensington Palace almost before (as the ungracious metaphor goes) the body was cold. Certainly at ever-chilly Balmoral there was earnest grief, but there was also a slowly growing sense of bewilderment at the magnitude of the communal mourning, and at the increasing demand for the queen to do something, say something—anything. Just as the Windsors had been mystified by and then resentful of Diana's immense appeal in her lifetime, they were again mystified by and resentful of it in her death. When Elizabeth didn't budge from Balmoral for days (the Palace claiming, certainly with justification, that Wills and Harry needed their father and grandmum at this time more than the public did), she was particularly savaged by the press for what was perceived as a deliberate effort to downplay the tragedy—to dis "our Di." Then she had a change of heart and issued a statement praising Diana and ordering that the Union Jack at Buckingham Palace be flown at half-mast. She finally made her way to London, and met with the grief-stricken outside the Palace. This did her a world of good with her subjects; whatever it might have done for her personally remains private—as does much else about Elizabeth II.

On September 6, 1997, more than a million mourners kept vigil on the funeral cortege route between Kensington Palace and Westminster Abbey. As the procession made its way toward the cathedral, one voice cried the sentiment of many: "We love you, Diana!" Others shouted "Bless you!" over and over. There was an overriding sense that this was a true tragedy, a tragedy of Grecian scale.

The late princess was, as we mentioned much earlier in our pages, buried on an island in a lake at Althorp. Peacefulness personified. For her, at least.

After a respectful period of mourning that might generously be called discreet, the Diana Saga was advanced by witnesses with poisonous points of view and, often, mercenary aims. Everyone who had ever been within perfume distance of the princess got a book contract. We could go on about this aspect of the Diana Industry, but we choose not to.

We choose, finally, to remember the woman: a remarkable, stylish woman with a unique gift, who used that gift to make many people happy, to comfort the sick or dying, to make us rethink how we should look at and deal with AIDS sufferers, to allow those of us with eating disorders to come forward and get help, to encourage us to hug one another, to encourage us to reach down and help a child, to encourage us to get involved, and to endure when the going gets tough. The historian Simon Schama, author of *A History of Britain,* among many other works, once referred to "the dark human comedy that was Diana's life

and death . . . where class met glamour and the result was catastrophe." That is true, certainly, but it is the broad-stroke view of Diana. Behind the constant drama—behind the tragic comedy—was a vulnerable, lovely, flawed, charismatic woman named Diana, who mattered to millions.

Why do we celebrate Diana Spencer on the occasion of what would have been her 50th birthday? That's an excellent question, and the answer each of us arrives at is worth pondering. That answer could be as simple as: We are all outsiders to the royals, and she was one of us. It could be: She was lovely, she was our princess. It could be: She did what she could to make the world a better place.

Also worth pondering, because this extraordinary life was ended at the age of 36: What might have been?

Diana, Princess of Wales
1961–1997